KRAKEN

Len Jenkin

BROADWAY PLAY PUBLISHING INC
New York
www.broadwayplaypublishing.com
info@broadwayplaypublishing.com

KRAKEN
© Copyright 2008 by Len Jenkin

Cover art: Pierre Denys de Montfort

First printing: April 2008
I S B N: 978-0-88145-298-3

Book design: Marie Donovan
Word processing: Microsoft Word
Typographic controls: Ventura Publisher
Typeface: Palatino
Printed and bound in the U S A

KRAKEN was first produced by the Todd Mountain Theater Project (Suzanne Pred Bass, Producer), opening on 7 July 2004. The cast and creative contributors were:

DAPHNE . . . . .Marisa Etchevarria
DEATH . . . . Zoe Jenkin
HAWTHORNE . . . . .Chandler Williams
MALKOVSKY, DESKCLERK, FATHER JEREMY
. . . . Joel Garland
MELVILLE . . . . .Jesse Lenat
SOPHIA . . . . Addie Johnson

In 1856, Nathaniel Hawthorne, author of *The Scarlet Letter, Mosses From an Old Manse, Tanglewood Tales,* and *The House of the Seven Gables* was living in Southport England, along with his wife Sophia and their children. He had taken employment as American Consul there. In November he had a visitor from America: Herman Melville, the author of *Moby Dick, Pierre, or the Ambiguities, Typee, The Confidence Man,* and the *Piazza Tales*. The two men had been close friends when they lived near each other in the Berkshire Mountains in western Massachusetts, but hadn't seen each other for a number of years. Melville was on his way to the Holy Land, a journey he hoped would help restore his physical and mental health.

Both men kept journals. Hawthorne recounts their time together in detail—a conversation on the beach, a visit to a cathedral. Melville says comparatively little about their meeting.

These two American writers, once so close, never saw each other again. The story of what went on between them during those few days remains a mystery.

The author's love and apologies to Nathaniel Hawthorne, Herman Melville, and Thomas Nashe.

CHARACTERS & SETTING

DAPHNE SHAUMBERG, *mid-thirties, English*
SOPHIA HAWTHORNE, *late twenties, American*
TURKISH DESKCLERK, *fifties, Turkish*
HERMAN MELVILLE, *thirties, American*
DEATH, *female, late teens, American*
NATHANIEL HAWTHORNE, *forties, American*
RUDOLPH MALKOVSKY, *fifties, English*
FATHER JEREMY, *fifties, English*

Southport England, on the sea near Liverpool

Joppa, a port city in Palestine

New York City

November 1856, and later

This play is dedicated to Quentin Anderson and Steven Marcus who, back in the Jurassic, sprouted me up from a tiny seed.

Where is God my maker, who giveth songs in the night?
JOB 35/10

Melville and I had a talk about time and eternity, things
of this world and the next, and books, and publishers,
and all possible and impossible matters...
Nathaniel Hawthorne

1.

(Southport. Sand dunes, a broken rowboat. Sound of the sea)

(DAPHNE, early thirties, sits in a beach chair. She has tattoos. She sips from a bottle.)

DAPHNE: *(Sings)* Haddock, plaice and porgy
Cod and mushy peas
I stroll the strand in Beulah-land
Doing what I please, ohhh, doing what I please.

(SOPHIA HAWTHORNE enters, late twenties, walking down the beach. She turns to the audience.)

SOPHIA: Its November of the year 1856. My name is Sophia Hawthorne. My husband is Nathaniel Hawthorne. The author.
We're from Salem, Massachusetts. At the moment we are far from home. England. A seaside town called Southport near Liverpool. It's the stupidest place imaginable. Liverpool is filthy, the lanes clogged with shameless whores and beggars.

DAPHNE: *(Laughs)* American bitch.

SOPHIA: Shut up, you.

DAPHNE: My name's Daphne, Sophia Hawthorne, and I'll say what I like on this beach.

SOPHIA: *(Under her breath)* Pathetic tramp.

DAPHNE: I heard that, my dear. I wouldn't be so quick to judge people, I was you.

SOPHIA: I don't need your advice, thank you.

DAPHNE: Don't you now? I happen to be a respectable lady. Mum was a milliner in the rows. My father, rest his bastard soul, worked for Jensens—when he was able.

Its no crime to like a fucking nip, is it? You look like one would do you good. Got no color in your cheeks, do you, darling?

(DAPHNE *holds out her bottle to* SOPHIA. SOPHIA *ignores the offer, turns back to the audience.*)

SOPHIA: I'm sick of being insulted by every drunk on this beach. It even happens when I bring the children. Una and Julian.

(DAPHNE *takes a long pull from her bottle, drains it, tosses it onto the sand...*)

DAPHNE: *(Sings)*
My father was the keeper of the Southport light
Fucked a mermaid on a moonless night
From this union there came three
A porpoise, a penguin, and the other was me...la la...
la la la, la la la la la...

SOPHIA: My husband was restless in New England. His old books weren't selling, and he wasn't able to find the inspiration for a new one. We grew poorer by the day. At last he called on his old friend Pierce. Franklin Pierce, President of the United States. They went to school together.

DAPHNE: What lovely luck...

SOPHIA: My husband thus became the American Consul in Liverpool, an employment to which he is particularly ill suited. Then again, there is no employment to which he is not ill suited, apart from writing and dreaming. When American sailors stumble into the consulate and beg for ten pounds he always reaches into his own pocket. I wish we could better afford it.

Southport is nothing but a waste of sand, with boggy pools to seaward. Old donkey-women and their scrawny animals follow people that stray along the beach.

DAPHNE: You know what they say? "Like a ride on 'em, dearie? Nicer than a man, and only ten p. Five for the kiddies."

SOPHIA: There are shipwrecks offshore. I went bathing one day with Una, and a corpse floated up to us in the surf. It had the bluest eyes.
I need to get home.

(SOPHIA *heads off.* DAPHNE *calls after her.*)

DAPHNE: Goodbye, my dear. Nice talking to you. See you here again sometime.

2

(*The Hotel Du Globe in Joppa, Palestine. Water in pools on the stone floor. Church bells in the distance.*)

(*A Turkish* DESKCLERK, *robe and pantaloons. His desk is covered with old manuscripts, and a number of cheap figurines of a man in a tattered robe. The* DESKCLERK *is occupied, clipping small pieces of his hair with a scissors, and gluing these little beards on the figurines.*)

(HERMAN MELVILLE *enters.*)

MELVILLE: Hotel du Globe?

DESKCLERK: Certainly. Hotel du Globe, in the holy and miserable city of Joppa, in the once great nation of Palestine.

MELVILLE: Sorry for asking the obvious, but there doesn't seem to be any sign, or any...

DESKCLERK: Ah. No wonder you are puzzlement. The storm. Last week. It blew every signboard in Joppa out to sea.

The reserve, sir? Name?

MELVILLE: Melville.

(The DESKCLERK *fumbles though a few letters of reservation, scans his book, at last finds* MELVILLE*'s name.)*

DESKCLERK: Ah, yes. God's will is good. Mister Melvilles. French, is it not? *Bonjour.* Mal ville. Sick town. How many days?

MELVILLE: I don't know. I'm waiting for a young lady to join me. A day or two. Or three. Or...

DESKCLERK: Whatever we can do to smooth the love doings, sir. Turkish apricot liquor, dates from Medjool, towels...

MELVILLE: That won't be necessary.

DESKCLERK: Pity. May I inquire the employment?

MELVILLE: Excuse me?

DESKCLERK: Your work. How you feed yourself?

MELVILLE: I'm an author.

DESKCLERK: Of books?

MELVILLE: Yes.

DESKCLERK: I also am literature man. Speciality of ancient manuscripts.

MELVILLE: Really? You...

(The DESKCLERK *comes closer to* MELVILLE*.)*

DESKCLERK: There's a certain fifth century Amharic scroll from Izmir that explains the terrible madness of Diocletian in this very city of Joppa, and what became of the jewelled hilt of his dagger, and the dream of that

papal dog, the leprous priest Luka Minchielli, who
pointed to the truth without fingers. And the curious
final chapter revealing the manifold and mysterious
guises of Death in this world.

(MELVILLE *picks up one of the identical figurines on the
clerk's desk: the bearded man, wearing a tattered robe.*)

MELVILLE: Who's this?

DESKCLERK: Jonah, of course. Here in Joppa, our patron
saint. Ten and six.

MELVILLE: Jonah's not a saint.

DESKCLERK: What does an ignorant Frenchman
bookwriter know about it, M'sieu Malvilles?

(MELVILLE *picks up an odd object from the deskclerk's desk.*)

MELVILLE: And what's this?

DESKCLERK: Beak of a squid. Big one.

MELVILLE: Kraken.

DESKCLERK: Some say. Sailors. A professor came once
from Jerusalem. He said it's only a shell, common one
in the Maldives.

MELVILLE: What do you say?

DESKCLERK: Best the Kraken stay in the sea.

(*Lights fade. Sound of a pen scratching in the darkness.
Lights up on* MELVILLE *in his room, Hotel du Globe. He
writes in his journal.*)

MELVILLE: December 19,1856, Joppa, Hotel du Globe
on the Mediterranean Sea. Unwholesome twilight. The
town is beseiged by an army of the dead—cemeteries
all around. Old Jew graves. The Hebrew inscriptions
can hardly be distinguished from the stone wrinkles
formed by time.
By the seawall below me, and farther along the

darkening coast, I can see the piers of Joppa, where
Jonah took ship to Tarshish.
She'll be here soon enough. In the time I have until she
comes, I want to write down what brought me here,
and about my friend Hawthorne and his wife
Sophia—the story of my pathetic stumbling journey to
the Holy Land.
*(He flips pages back in his journal. He reads, talks to the
audience.)*
Ah. October 1856, New York City. Sitting at my writing
desk in a black hole of misery. I'm ready to stick my
pen in my ear. Devil's in the inkwell and won't come
out.
(He picks up a book.)
Pierre. A dismal failure. Pointless.
(He throws the book across the room, picks up another.)
The Confidence Man. Even I find it unreadable.
*(He tosses it across the room, picks up another.) Moby
Dick*—a total failure.
(He tosses the book across the room to join the others.)
I dripped blood into those books. None of them sold
over three thousand copies.
I was so despairing and so angry that my own children
were frightened to come into my study and wish me
goodnight.
My wife Lizzie, desperate to get her fool of a scribbler
out of the damn house, suggested I travel, ease my
mind, find new inspiration.

LIZZIE: *(O S)* Go away! Far away!

MELVILLE: I love them all. They deserve better than me.

LIZZIE: *(O S)* Go to the Middle East. The Holy Land!
Jerusalem! Joppa! Come back when you're better.
More...like yourself.

MELVILLE: And with my head full of miserable
thoughts, I reluctantly boarded *H M S Glasgow*,
sailing from New York City to Liverpool, in the hope

that travel to the Holy Land would perform a miracle. I
was to return to my loving family in six months—a new
man.

3

(Boat horn. MELVILLE *at sea, at the rail in the evening.)*

MELVILLE: I hadn't been on the ocean for years. I knew
no one on board. Yet someone seemed to know me....

(A girl approaches MELVILLE. *She's young, attractive,
well-dressed. This is* MELVILLE's DEATH.)

DEATH: Mister Melville? Herman Melville?

MELVILLE: Yes.

DEATH: The author of *Pierre, or the Ambiguities*?

MELVILLE: Yes, but I...

DEATH: Interesting book.

MELVILLE: Thank you. You actually read the entire...

DEATH: Of course. I have all the time in the world.
Interesting, but tedious. Far too self-absorbed. In a
word—terminally flawed.

MELVILLE: Ah. But don't you think Pierre's inno...

DEATH: I'm from Pittsfield, Massachusetts, by the way.
I've seen you there on a number of occasions. In that
alley behind the stables.

MELVILLE: What are you talking about?

DEATH: I'm the chairwoman of the Pittsfield Ladies
Literary Guild, and we have a special interest in local
authors. We've read all your books. The Guild feels you
wasted the utterly prodigious talents granted you on
an overblown fish story no one understands. And then
there was *The Confidence Man*. Turgid philosophical

dialogues on a sternwheeler. Please.
Perhaps you're writing something new?

MELVILLE: A journal. I may base a long poem on...

DEATH: The dull adventures and speculations of a
number of fools in the Holy Land. *Clarel*, all in bad
verse. Unreadable.

MELVILLE: Have you been in my cabin and read my
notebooks? Who the hell are you? What gives you the
right to babble insulting nonsense to a man you don't
even know?

DEATH: I know you, Herman Melville. And you know
me.

(Long beat between them.)

MELVILLE: Yes. I do.
I can't say I'm glad to see you.

DEATH: Oh, but you are. You called me.
You asked God for comfort and release. Your pain
continued, and you felt your prayers went unheard.
Not so. God hears every prayer—and then forgets.
God forgets. I remember.
Its my job. I'm your Death.

(Silence, as they lean over the rail. Suddenly DEATH *points
out toward the sea.)*

DEATH: Look! There in the moonlight! About fifty yards
off. Something's rising up...that white blur...that twisty
pulpy thing floating on the waves.

MELVILLE: I've seen this once before. In the Southern
Pacific.

DEATH: Indeed. The great eye and endless tentacles of
God's own giant squid. Architeuthis, the deepest diver
of all. That one's huge.

MELVILLE: Kraken.

DEATH: Look, Herman Melville! Its sinking...
Its gone. *(Laughs)* Or was all that just a trick of the
moonlight on the sea?

(They look out over the ocean in silence.)

MELVILLE: Well? Is it my time?

DEATH: Do you insist on coming with me now?

MELVILLE: Where will I go? To Hell? To Paradise? To
some shadowy etern...

DEATH: I'm not allowed to say. Its a rule.

*(*DEATH *looks questioningly at* MELVILLE. *A long silence
between them)*

DEATH: I won't take you now. You amuse me. If you
write another book, it had better be a fine one.
By the way, when in Liverpool, see the American
Consul.

MELVILLE: Why should I...

DEATH: His name is Nathaniel Hawthorne.

MELVILLE: Hawthorne!

DEATH: *Mosses From An Old Manse* is an extraordinary
book—but not as good as you think it is. Gentleness,
solitude, and unhappiness aren't everything.

MELVILLE: My death is a literary critic.
What do I call you? Do you have... a name?

DEATH: Isabel.

MELVILLE: That's not funny.

DEATH: Not meant to be. Pierre's Isabel is my favorite—
a desperate sex-starved liar, longing to die—a lunatic in
a white dress.
You must excuse me. I'm a busy girl. I move to and fro
on the earth, and up and down in it. At the moment,

I'm having dinner with the Captain.
We'll meet again, you and I. In Joppa. Jonah's town.

(DEATH *is gone. Boat horn*)

4

(SOPHIA *at home. In another space,* NATHANIEL
HAWTHORNE *in his office by the Liverpool docks. A desk, a
U S flag*)

HAWTHORNE: *(Checking items in a ledger)* H M S Sea
Snake out of Liverpool: lumber, lamp oil, capuchin
monkeys, chinaware, saffron, scarecrows, steam
engines...

SOPHIA: I'm married to an extraordinary man. A writer
of stories. These stories take place in the past, with a
sweet melancholy about them—tales of the guilt and
terrible loneliness that live in human hearts. He's
writing a new one,*The Dolliver Romance.*
We're leaving soon, for a villa outside Florence...once
we have money enough to leave Southport behind. He
works well with that world around him—cypresses,
olive trees, houses of yellow stone. I will strip off my
clothes and lie naked in the Italian sunshine.
Meanwhile, from the docks of Liverpool, the ships go
to and fro upon the sea. Our American Consul is on the
job.

HAWTHORNE: *(Checking items in the ledger)* Sally Ann out
of Boston: calico, corn, cinnamon.
(He pauses in his work. He slaps the ledger shut.)
Horsewhips, feathers, blood, churches, vermin....
(He throws the ledger in a corner. He leans back at his desk.)
A poisonous sea creature learns to live on shore—
perhaps in a shoe.
A story, the principle personage of which is always on
the point of entering the scene, but never appears.

A fanciful citizen of Boston, once dead, has his burial in
a cloud.

SOPHIA: I am social enough, with American women
who visit, and with my occasional trip to London. I
walk in Saint James, drink claret, look at the pictures in
the galleries. Nathaniel has no friends in this country.
The few men he might call by that name are far away.

HAWTHORNE: A stray leaf from the Book of Fate, picked
up in the street.
Two persons to be expecting some occurrence, and
watching for the two principal actors in it, and to find
that the occurrence is even then passing, and that they
themselves are the two actors.
A person to catch fireflies, and try to kindle his
household fire with them. It would be symbolical of...
something.

SOPHIA: I worry about his health. Once autumn comes,
it's so damp and cold in this country, especially on the
coast. He's weak some days, with just strength enough
to go to work. Other days we walk for miles on the
beach.

HAWTHORNE: A demon wishes to amuse himself by
doing a good deed for a change—yet this deed turns
out to be more horrible than anything the demon has
done before.
A botanist, deeply immersed in the study of certain
poisonous shrubs... invents an odd leather helmet and
veil to guard against the deadly perfumes...

VOICE: (O S) Mister Hawthorne! Telegram!

5

(SOPHIA *and* HAWTHORNE *at home*)

SOPHIA: Well? Is Herman coming to dinner? Is he staying with us?

HAWTHORNE: I don't know. I just got his tele...

SOPHIA: You'll neglect to invite him.

HAWTHORNE: Perhaps he has other...

SOPHIA: Insist. He worships you. Otherwise he'll stay in a cheap hotel in Wandleigh Gardens, by the circus bandshell. He'll eat at a sad fish and chips shop, and arrive in the Holy Land with a stomach ache.

HAWTHORNE: I'll invite him. I'll go and...

SOPHIA: Jesus will welcome Mister Melville into the holy city, and Herman will reply by vomiting on the cenotaphs, on the wailing wall...

HAWTHORNE: I'll meet him at the boat, and drag him here.

SOPHIA: Lovely.

HAWTHORNE: In chains.

SOPHIA: Excellent. I won't have you sitting in that armchair, dreaming away the day.

HAWTHORNE: Dreaming is my business.

SOPHIA: The dream that matters to me is our life.

HAWTHORNE: I'm off. (*He exits.*)

SOPHIA: My husband has a tendency to forget to live. Mister Melville will change that for a few days. We haven't seen him or his family for years, since our time together in the Berkshires. Nathaniel and Herman were

up late into the night, talking about eternity and smoking cigars. He called my husband the Shakespeare of America. A bit much, even for me. Then we moved to Boston, and in the way men will, for no reason, they drifted apart.
Mister Herman Melville is a very excitable boy.

(Boat horn. A Liverpool pier. MELVILLE *is talking quietly with his* DEATH.*)*

MELVILLE: Emerson?

DEATH: Boring. A fool.

MELVILLE: What about Holmes?

DEATH: A greater fool. Already forgotten.

MELVILLE: Walt Whitman, Isabel? The poet who...

DEATH: Ah! Leaves of...something. He's a...

*(*HAWTHORNE *approaches.* DEATH *turns and walks away. She's gone.)*

HAWTHORNE: Herman!

MELVILLE: Nathaniel...

(They embrace, then step back, look each other over. They're both delighted.)

HAWTHORNE: Mister Melville, the pilgrim. Welcome to England.

MELVILLE: Mister Hawthorne, the American consul himself.

HAWTHORNE: And who was that extraordinary young woman?

MELVILLE: Who do you...?

HAWTHORNE: The one who just left.

MELVILLE: Ah. The daughter of an American adventuress. She and her mother are on their way to the White Mountains of Russia. From Pittsfield, actually. We met on board.

SOPHIA: *(Calling over)* Invite him.

HAWTHORNE: Herman, come to dinner.

MELVILLE: Delighted.

HAWTHORNE: In fact, come stay with us. Stay as long as you like. Forever.

MELVILLE: That won't be necessary. One night will do me, and then its on to Jerusalem, and if all's well, eventually Lizzie will have me back in New York—if I restrain myself from smoking cigars in the parlor.

(MELVILLE *and* HAWTHORNE *join* SOPHIA *at home.*)

SOPHIA: Boiled beef and parsley potatoes?

MELVILLE: Exactly what's wanted. And where's Master Julian, and the lovely Una?

HAWTHORNE: Still at school.

SOPHIA: It's so good to see you. How is Lizzie? And the children?

MELVILLE: Good. Better now, without me.

SOPHIA: Herman, is Lizzie...?

MELVILLE: She's taken Malcolm, Stanwix and the girls, moved up to Boston. Her father's house. Until I return. Pardon me, but I need to lie down for just a moment. I'm not used to sea voyages these days.

SOPHIA: Your room's upstairs, to the right.

(MELVILLE's *gone.*)

SOPHIA: Did he tell you? Why he's travelling alone...

HAWTHORNE: No.

SOPHIA: He's just on holiday?

HAWTHORNE: He didn't...

SOPHIA: For his health? To ease some nervous condition...

HAWTHORNE: He's chained himself to his desk. For years. Perhaps he just needs to...

SOPHIA: If ten years on that farm outside of Pittsfield didn't air out his brain, do you expect the Holy Land will? That serene camel ride to Giza, the stroll through Cairo with a crowd of beggars at his heels...

HAWTHORNE: Herman will never be happy unless he understands this entire universe and his place in it. Unless his mind becomes as wide as God's. I doubt that miracle will take place.

SOPHIA: Love trouble. That's why he's drifting about like a leaf. I'm sure of it. There they are, poor Herman and Lizzie, screaming at each other in the kitchen, heaving the china. Lizzie says Get out! Go to Egypt. Palestine! See the sand! See the...

HAWTHORNE: I don't think there's...

SOPHIA: How does he imagine Lizzie will care for those four children while he's gone?

HAWTHORNE: I have no idea.

SOPHIA: Ask him. Or I will.

6

(*The beach. The broken rowboat.* HAWTHORNE *and* MELVILLE)

MELVILLE: Have you noticed that this world is a rat's asshole?

HAWTHORNE: Welcome to Southport Beach, Mister Melville.

MELVILLE: Most people in it are raving madmen, or desperately unhappy. And this world of miserable people has made up its mind to shove me in a corner and put a duncecap on my head. I can't seem to persuade them to behave otherwise.
It's a simple fact, my dear Hawthorne. My books are failures, and all the blood in them would just as well have washed away.

HAWTHORNE: You brought those books into this world, and they'll outlive you, and me, and all your feeble-minded critics. If it was up to them you'd write *Typee* all over again, like an organ grinder's monkey, tipping his hat at a tug on his leash.
Work on something new.

MELVILLE: Why should I?

HAWTHORNE: Herman, you can't waste your...

MELVILLE: Waste is writing books if no one reads them—or buys them. Do you want my family to starve, Mister Hawthorne? Then send me back to my desk.

HAWTHORNE: When you finished *Moby Dick*, you wrote me. You said Leviathan is not the biggest fish—you'd heard of the Kraken—that great eye gleaming in the dark center of the world. It's still there.

MELVILLE: Not for me. I've tried again and again, and when each book is done it's a botch. The worst is, I care less. So does everyone else.
But scribbling is a hard habit to break. Passes the time. I'm beginning a journal.

HAWTHORNE: What sort of journal?

MELVILLE: Private. Of this voyage to the Holy Land. It's a strange uncertain business, poking about the world trying somehow to lift my own spirits. I miss Lizzie. And my children.
And you? Are you writing something new?

HAWTHORNE: I'm trying my hand at a sort of philosophical romance.

MELVILLE: What about?

HAWTHORNE: An old apothecary. A strange drug. The secret of eternal life. The usual things.

MELVILLE: And the title?

HAWTHORNE: *The Dolliver Romance.* I've promised it to Fields at the *Atlantic.* Monthly chapters. It's writing itself extremely slowly, what with Sophia, and the children, and the grand American consulship, which I should be extremely thankful for, I imagine.

MELVILLE: Extremely slowly. What does that...

HAWTHORNE: The thing was announced on the January cover. I sent off Chapter One. Two is now six months late. I hardly know what Fields should tell his readers. Ah—Mister Hawthorne's brain is addled at last, and much to our satisfaction, he cannot go on with *The Dolliver Romance.* We consider him finally shelved, and shall take occasion to bury him under a heavy article summing up his merits, such as they were, and his demerits, what very few of them can be touched on in our limited space.

MELVILLE: You'll get on with it. You have to. I intend to read it.

HAWTHORNE: I'm not quite up to writing these days. My strength is not what it was. Perhaps I had better keep quiet until it comes back to me.

(A silence between them)

HAWTHORNE: Do you need money?

MELVILLE: Not from you. I need to earn it. Lizzie's father has money if we get hungry.

(Sound of surf. MELVILLE *kicks off his shoes, rolls up his pants legs.)*

MELVILLE: I imagine I'm still able to walk on water. This English ocean will bear me up.
(He walks offstage toward the water.)

HAWTHORNE: *(Calling after him)* Pray for lightness!

(Sound of MELVILLE *splashing into the sea.)*

MELVILLE: *(O S)* Owwwww!

*(*HAWTHORNE *laughs. He imitates a man walking on the water, as if on a tightrope.)*

HAWTHORNE: Herman! Step on the curve of the wave! On the froth!

*(*HAWTHORNE *teeters side to side. Sound of a SPLASH!)*

*(*MELVILLE *returns. He's soaked head to toe, and shivering.)*

HAWTHORNE: Ye of little faith.

MELVILLE: Shut up. Ocean here is cold. Cold bitch of a country.

HAWTHORNE: Its not Italy. Or Palestine. Especially in November.

(They sit together on the sand. MELVILLE *shivers.* HAWTHORNE *puts his coat around* MELVILLE. *A moment's silence.)*

MELVILLE: If only I didn't feel so damn lost in this sorry world. Walking through Southport—the very cobblestones stink of gin. And that girl who came up to us—she wasn't more than ten years old. The fate of human beings breaks my heart. We face pain and death wide-eyed, like dumb animals, with no mercy to give each other. Our minds and hearts are torn, and never grow whole. Why does the God we pray to let us live this way?

HAWTHORNE: Ever since I've known you, you wander to and fro over these same empty deserts. There are no answers to your questions. Yet the world is still beautiful, my friend, dark places and all.

MELVILLE: Here in England, you've become a dim-witted country pastor. Reverend Hawthorne.

(A silence between them)

HAWTHORNE: The right reverend has two Cuban Riojas that need smoking.

MELVILLE: Ah!

(HAWTHORNE *takes out the cigars, they light up.*)

MELVILLE: Nathaniel, I believe my nerves are shot. I see things. Spirits.

(HAWTHORNE *laughs.*)

HAWTHORNE: I've been doing that since I was ten years old.

MELVILLE: I'm quite serious.

HAWTHORNE: So am I.

MELVILLE: This is not about characters who come, unbidden, to be in stories. A young woman followed me on this journey.

HAWTHORNE: Followed you? Are you...

MELVILLE: A very clever young woman, with a sharp tongue. She's read my books, for God's sake. All of them.
She claims to be my death.

HAWTHORNE: You weren't dreaming, or..

MELVILLE: You saw her. On the dock.

HAWTHORNE: I saw a young lady walk away. You said she was a...

MELVILLE: I lied.

HAWTHORNE: Herman, why should your death follow you? Are you ill? Do you...

MELVILLE: I brought my Death to me.

HAWTHORNE: And just how does one...?

MELVILLE: I made up my mind to kill myself.

HAWTHORNE: Herman, you're an idiot. Kill yourself, indeed. Listen to me. If every writer who was ridiculed by critics, or whose books didn't sell and fought with his wife, then killed himself, there'd be rivers of blood flowing down the library steps.
Herman, everyone loses faith at times. It will pass.

7

(RUDOLPH MALKOVSKY *the Bioscope Professor, fifties, with his equipment bundled on his back, appears. He sings as he sets up his bioscope show on the sand.*)

MALKOVSKY: (*Sings*) As I went out through Liverpool
To seek for recreation
One sweet day of summertime my mind was elevated
There were multitudes assembled
 And the tents were at their stations
My eye began to dazzle with the seeing them in rotation

Its there you'll see the strong men
At the fire and at the hoops
Men with long garters they call the Trick of the Loops
The thimble men so nimble, their fingers full of sparkles
And the splendid wheel of fortune
With its four and twenty quarters

Its there you'll hear the pipers
And the fiddlers competing
And the nimble footed dancers tripping on the daisies

They call for whiskey freely, they bow before they go
And they tickle the girls among the crowd
And their mothers never know
Tickle the girls among the crowd
And their mothers never know!

(The bioscope is a large box on a stand, with holes to look into, slots for large format glass slides, and a place to illuminate these slides from behind with lit candles.)

*(*MALKOVSKY, *his set-up done, turns to* MELVILLE *and* HAWTHORNE.*)*

MALKOVSKY: Gentlemen! The marvelous Bioscope. You no longer have to go there to get there.

HAWTHORNE: Some advice, my friend. We've been here all afternoon. Its dead. You'll set up your show and no one will see it.

MALKOVSKY: I've been amusing the British public on this strand for twenty years. I don't need to be taught my business by strangers. *(He puts out a sign:* BIOSCOPE TOURS, R MALKOVSKY, PROP.*)*

MELVILLE: What is that contraption?

HAWTHORNE: Old magic lantern show...

MALKOVSKY: Visit the great American West, the Rocky Mountains, and the Grand Canyon and never leave home. *(He holds up a large format glass slide.)*

MALKOVSKY: The touch of light to silver nitrate is God's breath into Adam's body—a miracle. See the monstrous buffalo, the cruel red men in their conical dwellings. See their naked squaws hanging out the family wash in the primeval forest.
Citizens of Liverpool need these visions special, as they live dead drunk inside an old rat's asshole. Any peep out they find remarkably refreshing.

HAWTHORNE: We're not from Liverpool. Americans.

MALKOVSKY: I spent a year there in my youth. New York, Providence, Boston.

(DAPHNE *enters upstage, carrying her beach chair. We can see more of her skin, and more tattoos.*)

HAWTHORNE: Have you been to Salem, in Massachusetts?

MALKOVSKY: Wouldn't go near the place, sir, I was you. Witch town. I'm Russian by birth, gentlemen, from Saint Petersburg. My mother was the Tsar's favorite whore.

MELVILLE: Why tell us these fairy tales?

MALKOVSKY: Fairy tales? As you wish, sir. But I'll tell you one thing. Everywhere I go, I study mankind. Americans, Russians, Englishmen, Hottentots. They're all the same. Mysteries. Every damn one of them.

(DAPHNE *sets up her beach chair.*)

MALKOVSKY: Daphne my mermaid, you've rolled out of bed. You owe me money. From last night.

DAPHNE: Shut up, Malkovsky. I'm taking the sea air with these gentlemen.

MALKOVSKY: My wife Daphne. Once in show business herself.
"View Miss Daphne Shaumberg, the Tattooed Princess in all her unashamed beauty. Her body is covered by luminous works of art. Ninety thousand stabs, and for every stab, a tear."
(*He makes a gesture of invitation toward the bioscope.*)
Homesick, gentlemen? Return to America.
Just give me a moment to bring in the crowds.
(*He goes off up the beach, crying out.*)

MALKOVSKY: Visit Hell through the magic of bioscopy! Naked demons torment naked sinners! (*He's gone.*)

DAPHNE: Malkovsky's never seen Russia. He's a Jew
bastard from Whitechapel. Had a pie stall in Brick Lane
till he discovered show business suited him better—less
work and more lies. Together ten years. We never go
anywhere, except to Swansea in September. To see his
Mum on her birthday. Stupid woman, fat and nasty.
She hates me. By the by, I don't have it off with
gentlemen. They don't appreciate love. Buy you a glass
of bubbly? Not them. They just want to get it over with,
go home to the wife.

MALKOVSKY: *(O S)* Naked demons torment naked
sinners with red hot pitchforks!

*(DAPHNE gets up, strolls down the beach. She reaches down
and picks up something off the sand. She holds it up. Its
small, and blue.)*

DAPHNE: Driftglass. The blue ones are the eyes of
drowned sailors. *(She's gone.)*

8

(Light changes. MELVILLE and HAWTHORNE alone.)

MELVILLE: Imagine the true Jonah, curled up in his
bunk as the ship to Tarshish shivers in the storm.
The sailors scream "God help us!" The sails are
shredded by the wind, and black waves crash onto
the deck. Down below, Jonah pulls the thin blanket
over his head. He's wet himself and the bunk stinks of
piss. He's failed God, failed himself. He's screwed up.
Screwed it all up. He wants only to be forever hidden,
to disappear.
The sailors chuck him overboard. The sea instantly
calms, the ship sails off toward the horizon, but there
is no great fish to save Jonah. His strength slips away,
and the cold sea drags him down. He breathes in the
salt water.His body dives deeeper and deeper into

unfathomable darkness. He drifts by the yellow eye of the Kraken, like a silhouette before the moon.

HAWTHORNE: The years haven't changed you.

MELVILLE: What does that mean?

HAWTHORNE: It means that you still spin your life into a web of doubt and unhappiness—as if God chose you alone to torment. You're not Jonah. You've done your best, and will do more.
There are no answers—that you haven't already been given.

MELVILLE: There are answers.

HAWTHORNE: No angelic being is going to take your hand, and tell you why women die in childbirth, and men break their bodies in the factories and with gin, and their children are born into sorrow.

MELVILLE: So we were made for ignorance, like sheep? We just wander about the world, and then one sunny day we double over in pain, lie down in bed and turn our faces to the wall. Is that it?

HAWTHORNE: There's only the winding road, my friend. Its why we need to love one another. Before we know it, the sun is already setting behind the hill, and the air turns cold.

MELVILLE: Blow the candle out, Lizzie, and let the darkness in.

(Sound of surf. HAWTHORNE looks out toward the sea.)

HAWTHORNE: Some days, out along the horizon, there's a curtain of mist. Behind it, the future hides. A wind parts that curtain for a moment, and I glimpse an army of shadows....
Another age is coming, a bloody time that will make this nineteenth century seem like Eden.

MELVILLE: I won't be here to see it.

HAWTHORNE: Neither will I.
I have a strange feeling sometimes about my stories. I
can't understand how I could have made them. I'm not
sure what they mean. They're like dreams, from a
childhood I can barely recall.

MELVILLE: Come with me. Nathaniel, come with me. To
the East.

HAWTHORNE: *(Laughs)* You know I can't.

MELVILLE: We'll solve the mysteries of time and
eternity under those silver-leaved olive trees, by
mosques with their spiked minarets, synagogues made
of mud tended by old men...golden light in the ancient
streets....

HAWTHORNE: Very pretty, my friend. But my life is
here, with Sophie and the children.

MELVILLE: In the souks of the A-rabs, we will lie
between the shadowy thighs of Bedouin courtesans
with their oiled bellies and hooked noses. These
diligent young women with olive skin will bounce on
our pale pokers. We'll become yellow-robed Pashas,
grow fat and sleek on dates and honey—our families
and books forgotten.
(He pauses. He's serious now.)
All right then. Stay home. I still intend to die there.

9

*(DAPHNE enters. Light changes. She takes a drink from her
bottle, sings.)*

DAPHNE: *(Sings)* Baby's in the cradle,
Brother's gone to town,
Sister's in the parlor
Trying on a gown,
Mummy's in the kitchen

Messing all around,
Papa's on the housetop
And won't come down

(MELVILLE *enters. He has his own bottle, takes a drink.*)

MELVILLE: Come down, Papa! Storm's on the way!
Blow you off that roof, up into the starry sky.

DAPHNE: Mister Melville.

MELVILLE: Brother's well out of it, isn't he? In town.

DAPHNE: Not really. He's drunk and dirty, hand in a
lady's purse. Or her knickers. Someone will stick him
and roll him in the mud soon enough.

MELVILLE: Nevertheless, an excellent song, Daphne,
depicting a moment of intense domestic panic.

DAPHNE: That number sounds remarkably smart at sea,
where I sang it to Captain Elias Mather of the Great Sea
Snake—a crack ship that sailed well with the wind close
on the quarter. She sank last year in a storm off the Irish
coast. Lost all hands. Except Captain Mather himself,
who, with God's help, clung to a spar. He was picked
up by the Rachel out of Bristol. Captain Mather spent a
week in prayer at Chester Cathedral, thanking God for
his deliverance.

MELVILLE: Who did he thank for sinking his ship with
all hands? If God saved Captain Mather, who drowned
the rest of them?

DAPHNE: Very clever, Mister Melville. I leave those
mysteries to the priests. I never look death in the eye,
if I can help it.

MELVILLE: We all do, at this life's edge—look down into
the dark.

DAPHNE: There's nothing in that darkness but your
own fears. Your own dreams.

(A silence between them. Sound of surf)

DAPHNE: There's an old donkey woman who lives in a shed out on the sandspit. She keeps a basket of skulls which she sets out along shore every evening to collect the gossip of drowned men. They tell her extraordinary tales from the very bottom of the sea.

MELVILLE: A good story.

DAPHNE: It's true. You can find her right up the beach. Near the pier. Completely bonkers.

(DAPHNE breaks into laughter, and MELVILLE laughs as well. DAPHNE stands, stretches, kicks off her shoes, takes some steps toward the water. MELVILLE stares at her.)

DAPHNE: I'm a mermaid, you know. A drunken mermaid. The high tide left me on the beach.

MELVILLE: I've always admired the beauty of full-figured women.

DAPHNE: Did you now?

MELVILLE: Even as a child.

DAPHNE: And do you still?

MELVILLE: More than ever.

(They embrace, and MELVILLE holds her tight. She's not unwilling. A long kiss, until DAPHNE pulls away.)

DAPHNE: That wasn't half-bad, now was it?

MELVILLE: No, indeed.

(He moves toward her again. From O S, MALKOVSKY's voice.)

MALKOVSKY: *(O S)* DAPHNE! GET OVER HERE, DAMN YOU!

DAPHNE: I'll give you some advice. For free. Listen to that friend of yours. Mister American Consul

Hawthorne. He's got a brain in his head, and he
understands you. You're on a high hobby horse, little
boy. Its got a switch tail, and its carrying you where
you little expect.

MALKOVSKY: *(O S)* DAPHNE! IT'S SHOWTIME!

DAPHNE: *(Under her breath) Shut up, Malkovsky. (To
MELVILLE)* I've got to go.

*(DAPHNE goes off, down the beach, away from the sound of
MALKOVSKY's voice. Crossfade to SOPHIA, in another space.
She sings, as if in church.)*

SOPHIA: *(Sings)* Let it shine on me, let it shine on me
Let Your light from the lighthouse shine on me
Let it shine on me
Let it shine on me
Let Your light from the lighthouse shine on me
When all my strength is gone
With your love I'll carry on
Let Your light from the lighthouse shine on me

10

*(HAWTHORNE and MELVILLE on the beach. The bioscope is
set up nearby. MALKOVSKY appears, crying his wares.)*

MALKOVSKY: See the towers of Trebizond! The
ziggurats of Uskadar! See the harem of a thousand
women of Sheikh Abdul Wahad the profligate....
(He spots something offstage, down the beach.)
Excuse me.

*(MALKOVSKY runs off. Sounds of a scuffle. In a moment,
DAPHNE is shoved onstage. She falls onto the sand.
She has bruises on her face and arms.)*

(MALKOVSKY returns, stands over her.)

MALKOVSKY: Daphne, my little mermaid. My loving wife.

DAPHNE: I'm not this bastard's wife.

MALKOVSKY: We had business. Where the fuck have you been?

DAPHNE: I'm not his wife.

MALKOVSKY: I could show you the papers, gentlemen. Rudolph Malkovsky and Miss Daphne Shaumberg, married at Swansea in the spring. Some years ago.

DAPHNE: I was fifteen. And intoxicated.

MALKOVSKY: That hurts, Daphne my dear. I still flatter myself that you loved me once. I'm a man, gentlemen, just like you. All the shit in my heart—it weighs me down.
You did mention you were authors?

HAWTHORNE: Yes, I...

MALKOVSKY: There's a bioscope discount.

MELVILLE: Both of us.

HAWTHORNE: Authors.

MALKOVSKY: Perhaps I've read something, some flagrant tidbit...

HAWTHORNE: My *Scarlet Letter* was published here in England. *Tanglewood Tales*—

MALKOVSKY: Kiddie book, ain't it? Saw it in a toyshop window. Good enough. You, sir?

MELVILLE: Here in England, two books. Some years ago. *Typee*. And then *Omoo*.

MALKOVSKY: The book about the cow. Loved it, sir.

MELVILLE: It's about the Pacific isl....

MALKOVSKY: You both qualify. Five shillings. Each.

(MALKOVSKY *takes their money, puts slides into the bioscope viewer.* DAPHNE *sits in her beach chair upstage.*)

MALKOVSKY: You know why I give a special rate to scribblers?

MELVILLE: Pity?

MALKOVSKY: Indeed. Members of a doomed profession, swimming in a stinking pot of egotism, syphilis, and envy. They write down tales that were fresh at the dawn of mankind, but have aged badly, and were dull centuries ago. All for an audience that grows more illiterate every day. For this, they expect payment. Sex. Love.
People only read books, as they drown in the saturating stink and sadness of their pathetic lives, because the very words, the simple black marks on the white page, remind them of the youth of the world. A quiet corner on a rainy day. The word is innocence.
However, people are less and less interested in innocence, their own or anyone else's.
The bioscope is hygienic, cheap, and amusing. We can make pictures of anything, and we will. One day these pictures will move and speak, and books will no longer exist. Friendship will no longer exist. Love will no longer exist. Just you, me, and the bioscope.

MELVILLE: To hell with the bioscope.

(MELVILLE *steps toward the bioscope, as if he might knock it over onto the sand.* MALKOVSKY *steps in front of him, pulls a claspknife from his pocket, flicks it open.*)

MALKOVSKY: Angry, are we? Mind your tongue, little man, or I'll have it out. You can't stand against progress.

(MELVILLE *doesn't back away.* HAWTHORNE *steps up alongside him.*)

(Two against one is too much for MALKOVSKY. *He laughs, closes the knife. He lights the candles to illuminate the scenes in the bioscope, makes a gesture of invitation.)*

MALKOVSKY: Gentlemen, see for yourselves.

*(*HAWTHORNE *and* MELVILLE *hesitate, then look through the two parallel peepholes.)*

HAWTHORNE: Is this a tree? A ghost?

MALKOVSKY: That's the Willamette Valley, with majestic Mount Hood looming, and that silver streak is the Colorado.

MELVILLE: The moon! Or is it Big Ben?

MALKOVSKY: Sunset on Lake George, with the sternwheeler American Belle.

MELVILLE: Big Ben! Six o'clock.

*(*HAWTHORNE *steps back from the bioscope.)*

HAWTHORNE: Scratched slides and a flickering candle. Nothing to see.

MALKOVSKY: The beauty of those landscapes so shook your senses, that all became a blur.
Try this.

*(*MALKOVSKY *changes slides. Again, they look.)*

MALKOVSKY: Both visions are the same. The Turkish Harem. The Bey Effendi prowling like a fat tom cat, fondling the breasts and buttocks of his many wives.

HAWTHORNE: In a crowd of rabbits...

MELVILLE: Those are monkeys. Or are they goats?

*(*MALKOVSKY *blows the candles out.)*

MALKOVSKY: We have returned to England. God save the Queen and the Duchess of York.

MELVILLE: Ten shillings back, if you please. We didn't see a damn thing.

MALKOVSKY: Is that the fault of the showman? Only yesterday Tom Tumble saw not only the Rockies of Wyoming, but the Mountains of the Moon. American scum like you should be thrown into pits, and eaten by sewer rats.

MELVILLE: Just return our money. I'm travelling to Jerusalem....

MALKOVSKY: A pilgrim.

MELVILLE: On a tight budget.

MALKOVSKY: Then go beg on the high road. Or ask God for your shillings. Perhaps he'll turn me upside down and shake the silver out of me.
In these times, my American friends, the unjust man doth thrive. It's a wicked world.

HAWTHORNE: Get yourself and this lying machine off the beach. Keep the damn shillings.

MALKOVSKY: Good enough! Daphne! Give the showman a hand, my dear.

(MALKOVSKY *begins to take down and pack up the bioscope.* DAPHNE *joins him. As she works...*)

MALKOVSKY: Mister Hawthorne sir, I could take you somewhere. Private. Meet some lovely ladies at a certain milliner on Bow Street, show a man what he needs to see. They'll even fuck a scribbler if the wind's right. If it blows in from the East.
Daphne spent some time there. Now her talents are available only to special customers.

DAPHNE: Malkovsky, I don't...

MALKOVSKY: Shut up, you useless bitch. (*Back to* HAWTHORNE) Perhaps the author of *Mosses From a Marsh* would like to step behind the dunes?

HAWTHORNE: No.

(MALKOVSKY *holds a finger up to test the wind.*)

MALKOVSKY: Ah, the wind is right. Admit it, sir. You could use a vigorous and charming fuck. Ten pound.

MELVILLE: Malkovsky, just let us be.

(MALKOVSKY *holds out a hand, begging for money.*)

MALKOVSKY: Please understand, gentlemen. We have to live.

(HAWTHORNE *and* MELVILLE *offer nothing.*)

MALKOVSKY: Ah, well. Come along, Daphne. We have business down the beach, under the pier.

DAPHNE: Go under the pier yourself. I'm in better company. Go on. Fuck off.

MALKOVSKY: Daphne, am I going to be disturbed on this road? Cut your lucky out of this, or I'll make you smell what you'd not like to tell.

HAWTHORNE: Let her stay.

MALKOVSKY: Even the American Consul can't step between a man and his wife, unless he wants one in the short ribs.

(MALKOVSKY *reaches in his pocket for his knife.* MELVILLE *steps in front of* MALKOVSKY, *joining* HAWTHORNE. *Stand off.*)

DAPHNE: Gentlemen. Please. I'll go.

(MALKOVSKY *laughs.* MELVILLE *and* HAWTHORNE *step aside.*)

MALKOVSKY: Its all very simple in the end.

(MALKOVSKY *loads the bioscope on his back.* DAPHNE *picks up the box of slides.*)

MALKOVSKY: The red hand of the devil spins the world. *(He moves off, singing.)*

MALKOVSKY: *(Sings)* Its there you'll hear the pipers
And the fiddlers competing
And the nimble footed dancers
All tripping on the daisies...

(DAPHNE lags behind. She blows the men a kiss, following MALKOVSKY.)

MALKOVSKY & DAPHNE:
They call for whiskey freely, they bow before they go
And they tickle the girls among the crowd
And their mothers never know
Tickle the girls among the crowd
And their mothers never know!

(They're gone. MELVILLE and HAWTHORNE remain.)

11

(The ancient cathedral of Chester)

(Darkness, candles, stained glass. The shrouded corpse of a child. MELVILLE and HAWTHORNE.)

HAWTHORNE: Some of the statues are curious. The entire church was...

(FATHER JEREMY appears out of the darkness.)

FATHER JEREMY: You've come for confession?

MELVILLE: Not today, Father. Tourists, I'm afraid.

FATHER JEREMY: We don't get many casual visitors. I'm Father Jeremy, the vicar here at Chester Cathedral.

HAWTHORNE: Nathaniel Hawthorne. I'm the American Consul in Liverpool. This is Mister Melville from the mystic mountains of Massachusetts.

FATHER JEREMY: You've come a long way. Follow me.

(They walk slowly down the nave.)

FATHER JEREMY: The cathedral of Chester is old.
Eleventh century. Old as pain. Old as blood. The walls
drip with praise of the Almighty—and the curses of
those denied by God.
Are you religious men?

HAWTHORNE: My wife Sophia asks me to church every
Sunday, when she takes the children.

FATHER JEREMY: Do you go?

HAWTHORNE: Never. I hate the praying, all the cold
pinched faces. The sermons are acts of stupendous
ignorance.

FATHER JEREMY: And you? Are you a believer?

MELVILLE: In my fashion.

FATHER JEREMY: I don't mean to pry. I only wish to
understand how honest I can be with strangers.
This great hulk of God's building lies abandonned on
the shore of the world. In the nearby streets of Chester
and Liverpool, life, such as it is, goes on.
(He moves to the child's shrouded corpse.)
A mother brought me this ten year old child yesterday,
wrapped in a blanket that smelled of piss. She asked
for a blessing to heal her. The brat was already dead
as a post. Stupid, pathetic prayers. I said them anyway,
in Latin. A small part of me hoped for a miracle—
that this cold child's eyes would open and she would
stir in my arms.
I am not the Christ. The child was already floating
down the River Lethe, small white bones splayed on
the worn velvet of its bed, rocked by the black waves.
Dead, and dying thus around us every day.
I ask you, gentlemen. Who watched over that child?

Her dumb, penniless, drunken parents? The rotting
towers of Chester Cathedral? God?

(Long silence)

HAWTHORNE: Can one smoke in church?

FATHER JEREMY: It's not allowed, of course. I don't care.
Let them put a pit for cock fights in front of the altar.

(HAWTHORNE *takes out a cigar.*)

MELVILLE: Perhaps God will curse you for that corona.

HAWTHORNE: We'll see, won't we?

(He lights his cigar. MELVILLE *points up at a stained glass
window.)*

MELVILLE: Who's that, in the window?

FATHER JEREMY: Jude. My particular patron. Saint of
hopeless causes.
Can either of you American gentlemen tell me why my
life here is so pointless? I can't help anyone who comes
to me, apart from empty consolations. Lies.
Do you know why there is so much suffering for
human beings? Poverty, sickness, death. People must
even weep in Paradise.
I look up at the starry night over the churchyard and
pray. GOD OF MY FATHERS! HELP ME! END MY
PAIN, AND THE PAIN OF THOSE I LOVE. I THROW
MYSELF UTTERLY ON YOUR MERCY.
This moment of total surrender to God's will is the
moment of total abandonment by Him. This moment of
turning to Him is the moment of His Silence, a silence
so infinite that no deed or prayer can change it.
Out of that silence, the saints alone can find their way.
The rest of us can't sleep at night, and we walk the
aisles of Chester Cathedral, clutching a candle, chanting
psalms under our breath. Our footsteps echo in the
stones.

MELVILLE: Saint Jude deliver us all.

(The child's corpse slowly rises under its shroud until it sits upright. No one sees this but MELVILLE. *The shroud slips off the child's corpse. It is* DEATH. *She looks directly at him.)*

DEATH: Mister Melville?

(She slowly walks toward MELVILLE.)

DEATH: Herman Melville?

FATHER JEREMY: The cathedral owns a silver reliquary from Constantinople. For years I believed it held part of the skull of Saint Chrysostom of Styria. A scientist visiting from London declared it to be the preserved beak of a specimen of Architeuthis. The Kraken. They say the Kraken could rise up out of the sea and wrap its arms around this cathedral, crush the towers, the nave, tentacles dripping blood down the stained glass windows...

*(*DEATH *is very close to* MELVILLE, *her arms outstretched toward him. He can't look away, or move...)*

FATHER JEREMY: I need to prepare for evensong.

*(*FATHER JEREMY, *his steps echoing, disappears into the depths of the cathedral.)*

MELVILLE: Father Jeremy! Father Jeremy!

*(*MELVILLE'*s voice echoes in the huge cathedral nave. There's no answer. His* DEATH *is almost touching him.)*

*(*HAWTHORNE *sits in a pew nearby, puffs on his cigar.)*

(Darkness)

12

(Late night at the HAWTHORNE's *in Southport.* MELVILLE,
HAWTHORNE, *and* SOPHIA. *They're all drinking
champagne.* SOPHIA *smokes a cigar.)*

HAWTHORNE: God condemned two angels into prison
for eternity, sealing them in the mountain of darkness
that separates Heaven and Earth. A traveling peddler
tells this tale to Henry Dickon, a storekeeper from a
small village in New Hampshire. Henry leaves his wife
and family and his little house by the river to search for
these angels, to discover what their terrible crime had
been.
He has no idea how to find the mountain of darkness.
He wanders aimlessly, living on the kindness of others.
Seasons pass, then years. He grows old. One day he
wanders back into his own village, but he doesn't
recognize it, and no one there knows him, with his
white beard and wild eyes. His wife and family moved
away long ago. He goes to the bank of the river, leans
back against a tree, and listens to the water. After all
these years, he's so very tired. His eyes close, and he
drifts into a dream...

SOPHIA: Oh, no. That's it, isn't it?

MELVILLE: Does he find the mountain of darkness? In
his dream?

HAWTHORNE: No idea.
Another. Whoever thinks the dead are the dead had
better think again. We are the dead—dying slowly,
rotting away, eaten by age, disease, and then by worms.
A young woman, Polly something or other, is taught
this by her embittered lunatic of a husband. The
knowledge poisons her life.

SOPHIA: She deserves it, pretty Polly. Listening to men, especially her husband.
Champagne? *(She fills all three glasses. A spill here and there. She's a bit drunk herself.)*

MELVILLE: One night Satan opened the gates of Hell and went out into this world to look around. While he was gawking at this and that, he vomited a black poison called aconitum. A company of beggars found this black stuff, and learned to make ink from it. They lay face upward in the fields, named all the stars, and wrote down poems and stories. These writers, for some meat and a few coins, made odes that promised people joy, and promised long life to the king. Then they'd run out of town before his majesty took to his sickbed, coughing blood. They're running still.

(Some laughter, and a silence)

MELVILLE: You know, in this travelling of mine, my sense of hearing grows sharper. I hear things—voices. They whisper to me from under beds in hotel rooms. In train compartments. Psychic effluvia, abandonned by prior travelers. Ghosts of loneliness, self-laceration, madness.

HAWTHORNE: A middle-aged literary tourist, crossing the Atlantic, perhaps on the H M S Glasgow, fancies that his pleasant travelling companion, an elegant young woman, may not be what she seems...

(MELVILLE laughs. He takes a Jew's harp out of his vest pocket, plays. His rendition of DAPHNE's comic song is wild, erratic, full of pathos.)

MELVILLE: *(Plays and sings)* Baby's in the cradle
Brother's gone to town,
Sister's in the parlor
Trying on a gown,
Mama's in the kitchen
Messing all around,

Papa's on the housetop
And won't come down
(He takes up a champagne bottle, drinks.)

HAWTHORNE: Herman...do you need some kind of help
from us?

MELVILLE: No one can help me.

SOPHIA: Really? How very special you must be, Mister
Melville.

MELVILLE: Sophia, I only...

SOPHIA: There is no one who can't be comforted by
another human being.

MELVILLE: I'm sorry, my dear Sophia, but there are
those beyond such comforting.

SOPHIA: If they shut out those who love them.
In the little church of Southport on Sea, where I
faithfully take Julian and Una every Sunday while
Hawthorne lazes in bed, the pastor tells us that
God loves every one of his children.

HAWTHORNE: In his dark and devious fashion.

MELVILLE: If God loves Herman Melville, you must
admit he has a hell of a way of showing it.

SOPHIA: Shut up, both of you. Have another drink.

HAWTHORNE: I will. And so will you.

*(HAWTHORNE pours champagne all around. They drink.
HAWTHORNE coughs, a hard wracking cough. With another
swallow of champagne, it stops.)*

MELVILLE: You know what I want from God? I want
God to talk to me the way a father talks to a child,
tucking him into bed. "I love you, little Herman. I love
you more than anything. In the morning I'll tell you
why the world is made the way it is, and what you're
to do in it. Now, its bedtime. Sleep tight. Have beautiful

dreams."
I call out to God from under the covers, but there's no
answer. I lie there, and my heart feels drained of blood,
and this empty heart shines like a mirror turned toward
my own face.
My Death is close to me, breathing gently in my ear.
She'll meet me on my journey, and I'll take her in my
arms.

SOPHIA: Herman, think of Lizzie and your children.

MELVILLE: They'll be better off without me.

SOPHIA: Christ. You're impossible. Do what you damn
please. Slit your throat on the Mount of Olives.
(She pours herself another glass of champagne.)

HAWTHORNE: You think you're done. You're not done.
Find your life again. I know you can, and I'm the grand
and wonderful Hawthorne you wrote that fat-headed
overblown review about. "The Shakespeare of
America," that's me—and I tell you there is more
for you to do.
It's a great thing to catch the fire even once, and let it
burn you down. You've done it. You will do it again.
And I promise you I will read that book, even in my
grave.
(He raises his champagne glass.)

MELVILLE: If I wrote the damn Gospels in this century,
I'd still die in the gutter.

HAWTHORNE: Herman, my dear friend, I've said what
I can say.
(He drinks, slowly leans back in his chair. He coughs again.
He's dead drunk. His eyes close.)

(MELVILLE sits in an armchair, lights a cigar. He watches as
SOPHIA manages to get HAWTHORNE standing. She puts his
arm over her shoulder.)

HAWTHORNE: Sophie—where are we going?

SOPHIA: To bed, my poor darling. We need to hold each other close, so far from home. We'll be so warm together, lying in the Italian sunshine.

(SOPHIA *walks* HAWTHORNE *slowly off to bed. They're gone.*)

(MELVILLE *alone. He smokes his cigar.*)

13

(DAPHNE *and* MALKOVSKY. *A cheap room somewhere near Southport. It's late.*)

DAPHNE: *(Sings)*
The admiral's on the lookout, spyglass in his hand
There's a pain beneath his heart he cannot understand
The morning sun is rising, blood red in the heat
It lights up a girl on her back in the street

And there'll be no more pain, no more tears, my
    darling
Everything broken will mend
When the ferryman comes home, my darling
All our sorrows will end

Mummy's at the cooker, she's stirring up a stew
Daddy's in the alley and he's doing something new
Sister's wandering down the tracks, on the edge of
    town
Devil's in the bushes and the night is coming down

And there'll be no more pain, no more tears, my
    darling
Everything broken will mend
When the ferryman comes home, my darling
All our sorrows will end

The girls have the babies, the boys have the drink
The boys have the best of it, that's what I think

Another summer's with us, another winter gone
I'm waiting by the seaside for the ship he's sailing on

And there'll be no more pain, no more tears, my
    darling
Everything broken will mend
When the ferryman comes home, my darling
All our sorrows will end

MALKOVSKY: Lovely sentiments, Daphne my sweet.
But...

DAPHNE: Shut up, Malkovsky. God will help the poor
man. And woman. Some day.

MALKOVSKY: I wouldn't trust the bugger to help
anyone. Little enough help he's been to me. Run over to
Mogg's and get us a quart of brown.

DAPHNE: Get it yourself. I'm not your dog.

MALKOVSKY: Yes you are. And a good dog too. Now
fetch!

(DAPHNE *doesn't move. Darkness*)

14

(MELVILLE *is still awake. It's almost dawn.* SOPHIA *returns
in a nightdress and robe.*)

SOPHIA: He's asleep.

MELVILLE: He drank enough champagne.

SOPHIA: He's missed you, you know. He talks of you all
the time.

MELVILLE: I missed him too. Mister American Consul
Hawthorne is not only America's most dark and secret
author—he's married to the most beautiful woman in
the United Kingdom.

SOPHIA: You're drunk.

MELVILLE: Possibly, but I'm prepared to defend my opinions with...

SOPHIA: We're not going to talk about your opinions, Mister Melville, or about your miserable feelings, or your misunderstood contributions to literature. Not now. I'm worried about my husband.
You know how solitary he can be?

MELVILLE: When the mood is on him...

SOPHIA: And how quiet, even with me and the children.

MELVILLE: He seems lively enough.

SOPHIA: He gathers all his strength to be with you. You don't see him day after day. He can be a whisper of himself. Lately he's lived more and more in dreams—I hold him close, but his mind is far away in some New England dusk, scarecrow in an autumn field...empty town square....
He grows weaker here in Liverpool. Less of him is in the world. I sometimes think a terrible secret gnaws at him, and then I find I'm only remembering his stories.

MELVILLE: Take him home.

SOPHIA: He won't go. We need the money he makes here. And we're to go on to Italy. To finish his book. Sometimes I worry myself too much—and then when he's weak or troubled or...
The world can be a fearful place. Without my husband, I don't know how I'd live in it.

(MELVILLE *is silent.*)

SOPHIA: I'm sorry. I know there's nothing to say.

MELVILLE: Take him to a doctor. Find someone who...

SOPHIA: He won't go.

MELVILLE: Sophia, I'd give him all the strength I have if I could do so. You know that, and he knows it. Tell him he's always in my heart, and I wish...

SOPHIA: You tell him.

MELVILLE: Not now. I have to go. It's a long walk in the dark to the Liverpool docks. My boat weighs anchor at six A M. The Egyptian, outbound for Genoa.

SOPHIA: Do you want me to wake him? To say goodbye.

MELVILLE: Let him rest. If I don't see him again in this world, I'll see him in the next.

SOPHIA: Don't talk that way. You will brighten as you go onward. Italy, Greece, Palestine.

MELVILLE: Of course I will.

SOPHIA: Death has wiser things to do in this world than pursue Herman Melville across the Atlantic.
My excitable boy.
We love you. I do, and so does my husband.

(She kisses him.)

(Boat horn)

15

(SOPHIA alone. She tips empty champagne bottles until she finds one with something left in it. She drinks it down.)

(HAWTHORNE enters, just waking.)

HAWTHORNE: Sophie, I was dreaming. In my dream the Wandering Jew came to Southport. He walked along the beach, ancient and slow. I rushed up to him on the sand. Then I realized—it was Herman Melville, white-haired, dressed in rags, travelling forever on the Wolf's Passport—on a pilgrimage with no end.

SOPHIA: I doubt Herman will find what he's looking for in the Holy Land. He needs to find his own.

HAWTHORNE: His own what?

SOPHIA: Holy land. The one in Palestine is sand and camel dung.

(HAWTHORNE *sits close to* SOPHIA.)

SOPHIA: How do you feel?

HAWTHORNE: Better. Melville's gone, isn't he?

SOPHIA: We'll see him on his return.

HAWTHORNE: You should have woken me.

SOPHIA: You needed the rest.

HAWTHORNE: Sophie, for years I was proud I wasn't one of those desperate authors who served up their own hearts, fried with brain sauce, as a treat for the public. I was wrong. I've never given enough of myself. I've never offered up the truth, my truth, the way Melville...

SOPHIA: Shhh. Of course you have. Young Goodman Brown, Ethan Brand, The Scarlet Letter...

HAWTHORNE: I've never given everything, shown everything. Even to you.

SOPHIA: My poor darling. You've given me so much. You can't help yourself, even though you want to hide so badly. That chain of human love and sympathy— it's there in everything you write, everything you do. It's twined round and round your heart.

(HAWTHORNE *and* SOPHIA *embrace.*)

HAWTHORNE: Sophie, I need some air. I'm going to walk on the beach.

SOPHIA: Perhaps you'll find the Wandering Jew.

HAWTHORNE: That dream's done. I have some ideas for *The Dolliver Romance* I need to think over.

SOPHIA: Would you like me to go with you?

HAWTHORNE: No need. I'm fine. Better than fine. Tell the children I'll be back by dinner time.

(HAWTHORNE *turns, walks off.* SOPHIA *looks after him.*)

16

(*The ancient port city of Joppa in Palestine.* MELVILLE *in his room at the Hotel Du Globe. He takes out his Jew's harp, plays for a moment, puts it away. He writes, reads from his journal.*)

MELVILLE: And so I've come as far as Joppa. Jonah's town.
No sleep last night—spent the hours cutting tobacco, hearing the surf and wind, waiting for her. Has she forgotten me?
Heavy fog everywhere, thick and raw. Down below, the old Turkish deskclerk, like a comfortable rat, surrounded by his little Jonahs, smokes away.

(*The* DESKCLERK *appears at his desk, puffs on his pipe.* MELVILLE *joins him. Sound of ship's bells in the harbor.*)

MELVILLE: Hear those bells? (*He looks out on the harbor.*) Impossible to see more than a few yards in this fog. The ships in the harbor must be terrified of smashing into each other.

DESKCLERK: God's will is good.

MELVILLE: The bottom of the sea is covered with the bones of men who cried "God's will is good" as their boats took water. The ocean doesn't care who drowns in it.

DESKCLERK: God's will is good, just the same.

MELVILLE: Have it your way. Any visitors for me?

(The DESKCLERK *puffs on his pipe, shakes his head. Then he holds up a little statue of Jonah from his desk.)*

DESKCLERK: Jonah. Cheap for a saint.

MELVILLE: Jonah's not a saint.

DESKCLERK: Indeeed he is, Mister Malville. Patron saint of drowned men.
Ten and six.

(Crossfade to MELVILLE's *room.)*

MELVILLE: The wind is rising, the ocean dashing itself over the sea wall. Foam on the beach like the slaver of a mad dog.
Ninety thousand stabs, and for every stab, a tear.
I'm sick of words, sick of speech. The chatter of empty-headed birds in hell.

*(*DEATH *appears silently, in semi-darkness, the same young woman* MELVILLE *met aboard ship to England.* MELVILLE *doesn't see her as yet.)*

MELVILLE: Lord, when shall I be done? It's a long stage, no inn in sight, night coming down, and the body cold.

*(*DEATH *comes into the light.)*

DEATH: We meet again, Herman Melville.

MELVILLE: I've thought about no one else these last days.

DEATH: I'm sometimes late, but I always keep my appointments.
Do you like Joppa?

MELVILLE: Its old. Damp. Narrow streets. People move around in it like flies in a skull.

DEATH: My kind of town.
It was good of you to wait for me patiently. I wanted to

give you time to consider the thing. Its rather final.
You called for me. The choice is still yours.
Do you want me to take you?

(MELVILLE *hesitates, and then...*)

MELVILLE: I do.

(DEATH *smiles.*)

DEATH: Follow me.

(DEATH *and* MELVILLE *leave the hotel room, past the
nodding deskclerk, out into the night. The fog is thick around
them.* DEATH *leads the way.*)

MELVILLE: Where are we going?

DEATH: Aboard ship. The ship to Jerusalem. I hear
you're a sailor, a good hand in a storm.
There ahead. The docks.

MELVILLE: Is that Jonah's pier, where he boarded for
Tarshish, fleeing...?

DEATH: Jonah's pier is dust.

MELVILLE: How do you know the way so well? In all
this fog...

DEATH: *(Laughs)* I'm the Captain.
There's our ship.

MELVILLE: Is it the *Pequod*...?

DEATH: The *Pequod* sailed and sank long ago. It's the
Rachel.
Take my hand.

(DEATH *extends her arm toward* MELVILLE. *He hesitates.
She pulls him in to her, wraps her arms around him.
They are one thing. Thick fog rolls in, obscuring the scene.
As the lights fade, sound of ship's bells.*)

17

(HAWTHORNE *walks slowly along the strand.* DAPHNE, *in her beach chair. She's got a bottle and a book. She waves him over.*)

DAPHNE: Mister Nathaniel Hawthorne! *(Holding up book)* Book of yours. Saw it in the market. I pinched it.

HAWTHORNE: Which one?

DAPHNE: *(Reading) Tanglewood Tales.*

HAWTHORNE: Those are stories for children.

DAPHNE: It's the same to me. I liked King Midas, and the one about the bears.
Where's your friend? Herman?

HAWTHORNE: He's gone to Jerusalem, Daphne. The Holy Land.

DAPHNE: Isn't Liverpool holy enough for him?

HAWTHORNE: He wants to... understand the world. Understand God.

DAPHNE: And good luck to him. On his return, he can whisper some of that understanding in my ear.

HAWTHORNE: And where's Mister Malkovsky?

DAPHNE: Gone abroad as well. Bioscopic opportunities. For an unspecified period of time. I'm on my own.

HAWTHORNE: How will you manage? I mean...

DAPHNE: Malkovsky left me money.

(A pause between them. Then...)

HAWTHORNE: Would you like to hear a story? Part of a book I intend to write. For grown-ups.

DAPHNE: Mister Hawthorne, tell away.

HAWTHORNE: Some years ago, a student of science invented a lamp. This lamp was fueled by human blood. In its light the student saw flickering shadows on the wall of his small chamber—shadows that showed him the shifting fates the burning blood had the power to reveal. Once lighted, the lamp would glow for as long as the one whose blood fueled it breathed the breath of life.

DAPHNE: Tell me the rest.

HAWTHORNE: I don't know anymore. Not yet.

DAPHNE: I do. He has a ladyfriend, your student. Its her blood. Isn't it?
Something will go horribly wrong. It always does.
Now I'll tell you a story. Malkovsky's dead. Thank God. I killed him. He was a cruel, disgusting, loud-mouthed, selfish toad. He never loved me. He pimped me, and robbed me. He made me have three abortions that ruined my insides.
We were in a hotel on the beach. The Edgewater Arms. I stabbed him in the chest while he was sleeping. His eyes opened wide. He could see it was me. He bled to death, all over the sheets. Hypocritical bastard. With his last breath, the *Shma*.

HAWTHORNE: *Shma...?*

DAPHNE: A hebrew prayer. Said in the presence of death. *(Sings) Shma Yisroel, Adonai elohainu, Adonai ehud.* I rolled him under the bed and checked out. Been weeks now. The hotel's closed for the season. Good riddance.
Don't think harshly of me. He was an evil son-of-bitch, though charming, and a devil with the ladies.

(DAPHNE *takes a sip from her bottle, offers a sip to* HAWTHORNE. *He shakes his head. She takes another.)*

DAPHNE: I wouldn't like to believe I made a mistake
telling you this. A girl has to take care of herself. Don't
you think so, Mister Hawthorne?

HAWTHORNE: Yes, Daphne, I do.

DAPHNE: You know, now Malkovsky's gone, my
fancy's returning. I'm not a girl who likes to wake up
alone. That's what matters, you know. Someone to
make the tea for.
Would you consider matrimony with a lively
Englishwoman of a certain age?

HAWTHORNE: I'm already married.

DAPHNE: Sophia. Leave her.

HAWTHORNE: We love each other.

DAPHNE: Well, then. Perhaps we could fall into bed
together some rainy afternoon.

(HAWTHORNE *laughs. He takes out two cigars, offers one to*
DAPHNE.)

HAWTHORNE: Do you smoke?

DAPHNE: I believe a lady can enjoy a cigar.

(They light up. They smoke.)

DAPHNE: A giant squid washed up on the beach
last night. Right by the pier. It might have been dead
for days, just floating in the waves. The people of
Southport are gathered all round it, cutting off parts
for souvenirs. Most of the tentacles are already gone. I
thought you, or your friend Herman, might be....

(HAWTHORNE *coughs, then suddenly doubles over in pain,
an expression of agony on his face.)*

DAPHNE: Mister Hawthorne? Are you...

HAWTHORNE: *(With effort)* I'm all right. It'll pass. *(He slowly straightens, barely able to stand upright. He's still in pain, confused.)*

DAPHNE: You need to sit, Mister Hawthorne. Easy...

(DAPHNE helps HAWTHORNE into her beach chair. He sits, breathing heavily.)

DAPHNE: Do you know what's wrong with you?

HAWTHORNE: It happens sometimes. Pain in my chest, and then weakness—the world seems like shadows till its gone.
I'm a bit better now...

DAPHNE: You don't look better—pasty white you are. You better let your wife tuck you in.

HAWTHORNE: I need to go home.

(HAWTHORNE struggles to his feet. He's unsteady, and DAPHNE helps him. He starts to walk away.)

DAPHNE: Leave me some money.

HAWTHORNE: What for?

DAPHNE: For my company.

(He turns back, hands her some money. He leaves, walking with effort.)

(DAPHNE watches him go. She sips from her bottle. She sings.)

DAPHNE: *(Sings)* Baby's in the cradle
Brother's gone to town,
Sister's in the parlor
Trying on a gown,
Mummy's in the kitchen
Messing all around,
Papa's on the housetop
And won't come down

18

(SOPHIA. HAWTHORNE lies in bed near her, under covers. Sound of the sea. She reads to him.)

SOPHIA: *(Reading)* Chapter sixteen. The country road they traveled entered the city by a winding street. There was no moon, and few stars. It was that preluding hour of the night when the shops are just closing, and the aspect of almost every wayfarer, as he passes through the unequal light reflected from the windows, speaks of one hurrying not abroad, but homeward...

(SOPHIA looks closely at HAWTHORNE to see if he's fallen asleep. He has. She puts down the book, straightens his covers.)

SOPHIA: He walked home from the beach. As soon as I saw his face I was frightened—so pale. His brow was streaming with sweat. I put him to bed, and read to him all that evening and after he woke this morning. From Herman Melville's *Pierre*.

HAWTHORNE: Sophie...water. Please.

(She brings it to him. She supports him, holding him in a sitting position so he can drink.)

HAWTHORNE: Pen and paper. I need to write. A letter to Herman, so he won't...hurt himself...among strangers.

SOPHIA: I'll do it, darling. I'll write to him.

(She lowers him to the pillow.)

SOPHIA: Sleep now. Rest.

(SOPHIA takes up pen and paper, sits in a corner of the room, writes the letter to MELVILLE. HAWTHORNE breathes heavily. Out of the deep shadows, the figure of DEATH

appears. HAWTHORNE *senses her presence. He struggles to sit up in bed.)*

DEATH: I'm reading your notebooks. It's a pleasure, Mister Hawthorne, to hear you talk to yourself.

HAWTHORNE: Those pages are private. I've never...

DEATH: I've even read *The Dolliver Romance*, what there is of it. A drug to become young again—please. Editor Fields of the *Atlantic Monthly* sits at his desk, his flesh becomes dust, and his white bones wait for a new chapter to arrive in the post. It never will.

HAWTHORNE: I've seen you before... on the beach. You're from Southport...

DEATH: Of course I am. Now two white deer stand at the edge of the sea. The hour is struck. Shall we go?

HAWTHORNE: Sophie! Sophie...

(SOPHIA *writes on. She can't hear him. He's already in another world.* DEATH *sings...)*

DEATH: *(Sings)* Brightness falls from the air
Queens have died, young and fair
Come, come, the bells do cry
All who live, all must die

HAWTHORNE: I know who you are.

DEATH: Of course you do. I know you, Nathaniel Hawthorne, and you know me.

(DEATH *steps forward, seems to grow larger. She stretches an arm toward* HAWTHORNE, *covers him with her dark shadow.* HAWTHORNE *lies still.)*

(DEATH *is gone.)*

SOPHIA: My husband died in his sleep. He died in a dream of some sweet and strange past. A scarecrow stirs in a New England breeze. An Italian summer, where we lay together on a hillside above Florence

and the air smelled of rosemary. Nathaniel said
"Sophie, look!" and it was a single swallow, circling
overhead, a black speck in the blue immensity.
Don't wake him. None of you must wake him.

(SOPHIA *touches the dead face of* HAWTHORNE.)

SOPHIA: So cold.
I need to warm the ice in his blood, and make him
ready for his mournful journey to heaven.

(SOPHIA *embraces* HAWTHORNE's *dead body.*)

19

(*Light changes.* SOPHIA *walking on the beach at Southport.*
DAPHNE *in her beach chair.*)

(SOPHIA *pauses.* DAPHNE *takes a sip from her bottle.*
She stands, takes a step toward SOPHIA.)

DAPHNE: I'm sorry to hear about your husband, Sophia
Hawthorne. I would see him here on the beach. He
reminded me of a quiet king in a fairy tale.

SOPHIA: Thank you.

DAPHNE: Is there anything I can do for you?

SOPHIA: I appreciate your kindness, but...

DAPHNE: Would you like a drink?

SOPHIA: I believe I would, thank you.

(DAPHNE *passes* SOPHIA *her bottle, and* SOPHIA *takes a*
long sip. She offers the bottle back to DAPHNE.)

DAPHNE: Keep it. There's more where that came from.

(DAPHNE *walks slowly off down the beach. She's gone.*
SOPHIA *alone. She takes another sip.*)

SOPHIA: Mister Herman Melville didn't die in a hotel
room in Joppa. In the end, he didn't kill himself—

or his Death wouldn't take him.

He returned from the Holy Land to his wife and family
in New York. Just as Nathaniel had done in Boston, he
worked in the Customs House for years, weighing,
stamping, affixing the seal of the United States to goods
from far-off lands.

Herman Melville, the excitable boy—even he grew old.
His beard grew long and his writing grew worse,
boring and pointless. At the end they found the story of
Billy Budd, Sailor in his desk, and it was touched with
the old fire.

20

*(Twenty-sixth Street, New York City, many years later.
MELVILLE at his desk. He's an old man, and his hair is white.
The manuscript of* Billy Budd, Sailor *is in front of him.
He makes some changes, reads aloud to himself.)*

MELVILLE: Fathoms down, fathoms down,
How I'll dream fast asleep
I feel it stealing now. Sentry, are you there?
Just ease these darbies at the wrist,
And roll me over fair!
I am sleepy, and the oozy weeds about me twist.
(He puts the manuscript in his desk drawer.)

*(DEATH appears, looking as young as she did in Joppa many
years ago. She steps out of the shadows.)*

MELVILLE: I've been expecting you, Isabel.

DEATH: I hope I haven't kept you waiting long. By
the way, I'm sorry about that remark I made years
ago about an overblown fish story. I've done some
re-reading since then. The whale book does honor
to this world, and all the creatures in it.

MELVILLE: I'm afraid you exagggerate.

DEATH: Not at all. For a few years in the Berkshires you were the equal of Shakespeare. Not Hawthorne. You. The last time we met, in Joppa, at the final moment, you chose to live. How have the years been to you?

MELVILLE: Like the years of other men who grow old. Some great joys...and some days there are always tears right behind my eyes, as if I'm in mourning—for a life that could have been—where I knew more, gave more, loved more...

DEATH: Ninety thousand stabs, and for every stab, a tear.
You've lived. More than most.

MELVILLE: Do you pity me at all?

DEATH: I pity everyone—the doomed babe in its cradle, and white-haired Herman, whose feet already falter on the hill.
I know you finished the book. The last one.

MELVILLE: Its called *Billy Budd, Sailor.*

DEATH: I've read it. You should be proud.
"Fathoms down, fathoms down
How I'll dream fast asleep..."

(DEATH *steps toward* MELVILLE. *She seems to grow larger...*)

DEATH: Is there any last gift I can give you?

(MELVILLE *is quiet for a long moment.*)

MELVILLE: Yes. I want to see them again, one more time, though they died long ago. The Hawthornes. Nathaniel and Sophia.

(*Light changes.* HAWTHORNE *and* SOPHIA *appear in the distance, walking along the beach.*)

DEATH: Dawn on the beach at Southport. The sea is calm and the new sun streaks it gold. Sophia bends down to pick up a piece of blue driftglass, and the

retreating foam of the waves brushes her fingers. A chill
that moves through her body for a moment. Nathaniel
takes her hand.
They dissolve in the light that comes streaming off the
sea. The ocean smells like blood and wrack and tide...

(HAWTHORNE *and* SOPHIA *are gone.*)

(*A white light in* MELVILLE's *room.* DEATH *stands by him at
his desk.*)

DEATH: Let's go, shipmate. All aboard for the Southern
seas. I am the Captain, the Kraken herself, your true
love—and now I take you with me at last.

(DEATH *reaches out and touches* MELVILLE, *then covers him
with her dark shadow. The light fades.*)

(MELVILLE *slumps over his desk, motionless.*)

(DEATH *is gone. Silence. Boat horn*)

21

(DAPHNE *on the beach, alone. She takes a nip from her bottle,
sings.*)

DAPHNE: (*Sings*) Haddock, plaice and porgy
Cod and mushy peas
I stroll the strand in Beulah-land
Doing what I please, ohhh, doing what I please.
(*She takes another drink.*)

(*The beach is streaked with golden light. Then darkness...*)

EPILOGUE

DEATH: Our actors commend themselves to you, and they humbly beg your pardon if their tongues stumbled unwittingly into anyone's happiness. It's rare enough in this world. Tonight these hammer-headed clowns have played the lives of great authors long dead and in their graves in a dance here before you. As I am Death herself, I ask you to love them, with their faults. In any heap of coins, you'll find a piece of silver, even gold. Pay for the evening's sport with your applause, and when the dark wind blows in your direction, I will find myself some business on the other side of the world. Goodnight, ladies and gentlemen.

END OF PLAY